IMAG

Oldham

Curzon Street in the 1960s. Ardern's curtain shop awaits the takeover by Trilby, owned by Peter Haq.

IMAGES OF ENGLAND

Oldham

Freda Millett

NONSUCH

Union Street, c. 1910.

First published 1996
This new pocket edition 2005
Images unchanged from first edition

Nonsuch Publishing Limited
The Mill, Brimscombe Port,
Stroud, Gloucestershire, GL5 2QG
www.nonsuch-publishing.com

British Library Cataloguing in Publication Data.
A catalogue record for this book is available from the British Library.

ISBN 1-84588-164-8

Typesetting and origination by Nonsuch Publishing Limited
Printed in Great Britain by Oaklands Book Services Limited

Contents

Goodbye to one of Oldham's greatest assets: Buckley and Prockters, demolished in 1961.

Introduction

Samuel Pepys said 'Listen to what I write because tomorrow everything will be changed'.

Look at a map and you will see Oldham seven miles north-east of Manchester city centre. It seems merely to be a part of Greater Manchester – one of ten cities and towns in which map-grey housing and industry merge in a densely packed mass of three million or so souls in the North-West's most vibrant and lively conurbation.

But if you thought that any of the towns around the twin cities of Manchester and Salford would be happy with that description you would be wrong. Few of them would be content to be thought of as being part of Greater Manchester. All are fiercely independent, perhaps none more so than Oldham. That is not surprising. After all, it was not only a Lancashire mill town – in its heyday it was the greatest cotton spinning and textile machinery-making centre the world has ever seen. At its height, there were 320 cotton-spinning mills in Oldham and its surrounding districts of Shaw, Chadderton, Royton, Failsworth and Lees. This was raw industry on an incredible scale which will never be matched in this country again. Those not used to seeing the total dedication to the production of one commodity and the making of machinery to allow that to be possible found Oldham almost overpowering.

The mills stand cheek by jowl with dwellings, hotels, perhaps even churches, in a way that must be seen to be believed. Within a few yards of the town hall you can hear the low purring growl of caged machinery, and the smoke of the innumerable tall chimneys lies over all like a poultice... Brick houses and shops go on for ever, and at the back of them, blotting out all the rest of the world, rise great precipitous mills, like frowning cliffs at whose base are the small houses where the folks live like coneys at a mountain foot.

That, believe it or not, was not the view of a visitor from elsewhere in the country or abroad. This description appeared in a newspaper published in 1908 only a few miles from Oldham in Manchester.

The huge expansion which saw Oldham explode from a small town enjoying the fruits of the Industrial Revolution to a cotton-spinning Leviathan sucked in people from all over the country. Its population reached a peak of 163,000 in 1911, not including the out-districts which added tens of thousands more to this total. It is mostly gone now, of course. The great textile machine-makers, like Platt Bros, died. The cotton-spinning companies died, too. Now only four mills are still spinning cotton. The illness of under-investment, cheap imports and disappearing export markets was long and painful. Some are not sad to have seen it disappear. After all, Oldham might have been great, but for most it was not a pleasant place to live.

Though some have fond memories of the community spirit in the acres of cheap terrace homes built to house mill-workers as they poured into the town to earn a living at the beck and call of the factory hooter, we should never forget that it was a community spirit born in many cases of terrible adversity.

Some would wipe out those memories, but we cannot afford to forget. The greatness of Oldham's past is why most of the population is living here today, even though they are descendants of those who first abandoned the land and even their country to work in the mills. And the last of those waves of workers arrived only in the 1960s and 1970s – the Indian, Pakistani and Bangladeshi communities that now make up about 9 per cent of Oldham's population.

It is why I am here. In 1855, my schoolmaster-turned-journalist great great grandfather left his job as leader writer of the *Huddersfield Examiner* to become editor of the *Oldham Chronicle* in a growing town that was thirsting for news about itself. He and a partner bought the newspaper for £800 a couple of years later, and my family have been running it ever since.

Roots are important. They say that if you don't know where you have been, you don't know where you are going, and that is why books like this are more than simply enjoyable for their quaint snapshots of time gone by. They allow us to attempt to grasp the past and give us a sense of continuity.

Perhaps no one is better equipped to make the selection of photographs from the thousands available than Freda Millett. As the former curator of Oldham's museum, there are few people I know who have such a genuine sense of place and sincere love of their home town and its people. She even managed to persuade me that the *Chronicle* itself deserved a chapter. She was right. As the town's main source of news for over 140 years, perhaps it does no harm to peep into its past, though the many thousands of people who have appeared in its pages in words and in pictures that capture sadness and joy, triumph and failure, good and evil will always be the newspaper's most enduring testament.

Here I have tried to explain why I think that this little book is important, even though its captured moments are fleeting and perhaps trivial, but you don't have to believe me. You don't have to sit down and contemplate the tides of time which washed me and perhaps you on to Oldham's shore.

Simply enjoy it.

Philip Hirst
Editor, *Oldham Evening Chronicle*
July, 1996

One

Another Kind of Shopping

Window dressing for many of the shops in Oldham was a great challenge with prizes awarded regularly. Here, Meadow Dairy on Curzon Street competes.

OLDHAM
BANK OF HEALTH,
MARKET PLACE.

WILLIAM DEWHIRST,
CHEMIST, & DRUGGIST, MANAGER,

Begs to invite the attention of the Public, and in particular those parties, who are suffering from the usual complaints to which common humanity is ever liable.

The Oldham Bank of Health

Offers a sure refuge to the afflicted, where they may deposit their money with safety—where a double amount of interest to themselves may be secured, and an assurance of obtaining sound and experimental advice, with the most appropriate remedies. Having received from the successful treatment of various disorders the most flattering testimonials, the Proprietor of the

OLDHAM BANK OF HEALTH,

Is thus induced to make known the following remedies, which he can confidently Recommend :

Tamarind Cough Mixture,

This most unparalleled remedy has given universal satisfaction, in cases of Cough, Hoarseness, difficulty of breathing, obstruction of the lungs and old asthmatic complaints.

FAMILY PILLS,

For disorders of the head, Stomach, and Bowels, and when a good Purgative is wanting these Pills are excellent.

INFALLIBLE PILE POWDERS.

These Powders have without exception performed wonderful cures in the most distressing case of Piles. They give immediate relief, and in a few days the Piles disappear without return.

RING WORMS

Effectually cured in a few days by one or two applications None need be troubled with Ring Worms.

TOOTH ACHE TINCTURE,

which is allowed to be the best, safest, and most immediate cure for Tooth Ache, often rendering extraction needless.

Also a many other remedies too numerous to be inserted here, such as for Itch, Swelled Necks, Canker, Scalded Head, Cholera, Bowel Complaint, Flux, Hooping Cough, Croup, Teething, Worms, &c.

Medical or Kitchen Porter.—Burning Naptha.

Hair Oil, Castor Oil, Tincture Rhubarb, Godfrey's Cordial, also, Paints, Colours, and every Drug that is usually sold, may be obtained at the

Oldham Bank of Health.

Teeth carefully extracted and decayed ones stuffed.

Wholesale Dealers supplied on the lowest terms.

N.B. W. D. gives Change for a Shilling.

Robinson's stall in the Victoria Market Hall in the 1940s.

Victoria Market Hall in 1974, just before the fire which destroyed it, looking towards the Albion Street entrance and exit. The coat of arms can be seen cut out in wrought iron above the heads of the shoppers.

Equitable Co-op shop on Abbeyhills Road in the late 1940s.

King Street in the 1920s looking towards the Star Inn, with all the splendour of the Co-operative buildings on both sides of the road.

The upper storey of shops on Yorkshire Street collapsed in May 1947. The area affected was once known as Braddock's Assembly Rooms where dances and concerts were held around the turn of the century. For a brief time, before the Town Hall was built, the rooms were also used for council meetings. The basement under the shops was the beginning of Oldham's first indoor market.

The Grey Horse Inn, Union Street, tucked away between two buildings in 1930. It was pulled down for the erection of the 'new' Grey Horse which extended to the corner and was across the way from the Grosvenor Cinema.

Victoria Market Hall in the 1970s; 'Everything under one roof'.

Although the retail outlet no longer exists, Giles Shaw and Company still stands at No.72 Manchester Street. This is one of the oldest established firms in the town. The business was founded in 1833 by John Barstow and taken over by Giles Shaw in 1865. Many of Oldham's mills were fitted with gas and steam by Shaws who specialised in builders' ironmongery.

The confectioner's shop in this photograph was on Manchester Street, almost where the turning is now for Sainsburys. It was always called the 'run down' because when you went in, you actually had to run in the shop because the floor sloped so suddenly. I knew someone who was friendly with the people who lived there and upstairs you couldn't stand up, the ceiling was so low!

Challinor's confectionary and grocers business at No.19 Huddersfield Road. This photograph, taken in 1884, shows three generations of the family outside the shop.

Opposite above: The Donnelys had Nos 3, 5 and 7 Henshaw Street for their mixed business and butchers in 1900. They also had a shop in the Victoria Market Hall.

Opposite below: Tommyfield Market in 1900.

Peter Street, c. 1935. This area is one of the exits from what is now Spindles car park.

The High Street in 1935. Irlam's café advertises a four course lunch for 1/6 (7½p).

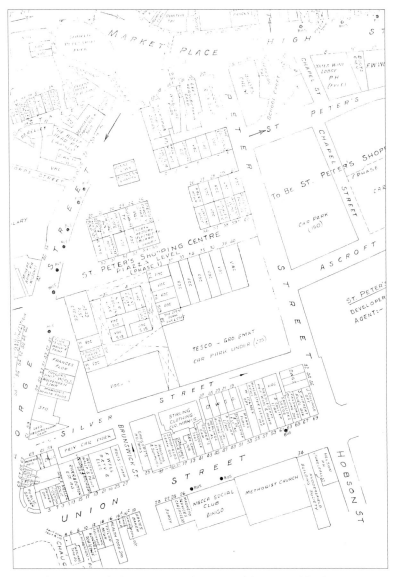

A map showing St Peter's shopping centre, phase one and the extent of the shops on Union Street in 1973.

Oldham Industrial Co-operative Society wagon decorated for the parade, with children sitting underneath the advertising. The wagon was photographed in Foundry Street with the Co-op offices in the background.

The High Street in the 1960s.

Two

Let's Follow the Band

Whit Friday, and schoolchildren pass Rhodes Bank in 1925.

Oldham Postal Band, outside the general post office in Greaves Street in 1908.

Horse and cycle parade passing along Rochdale Road, Oldham. Part of Whatmough's hat shop at the bottom of Barker Street can just be seen on the right.

Horse and cycle parade in 1908.

'We lived in Glodwick, so we saw the horse and cycle parade on its way back to the park. Our cousins and aunts and uncles all came for tea. We got buffets and chairs near the kerbstone and we sat all afternoon, waiting. What I remember most are the horses with shining brasses, their tails and manes plaited and tied with bows and coloured ribbon.'

The Victory Parade in 1945 seen by spectators outside the Town Hall. The man in the raincoat on the left of the photograph is the late Dr Kelso (Senior) with his son Tom and Mrs Kelso on his left. The Mayor was Stirling Marron JP.

Crowds watching the 1945 Victory Parade at the Town Hall.

The memorial procession for Edward VII passes Central Baths on Union Street in 1910. The General Post Office, now the Local Studies Library, can be seen in the background. The Bluecoat boys march in front of Dame Sarah Lees and the mayor.

Oldham Territorials leave their town and loved ones in August 1914 to fight in a war they knew very little about. This photograph shows them marching to the station. It was very early in the morning which accounts for the lack of spectators.

Large crowds turned out to cheer the survivors of the Oldham Territorials in April 1919 as they marched from Clegg Street Station, across Union Street, on their way to the Drill Hall on Rifle Street. Some hearts would be heavy as they recalled that grey morning in August 1914 when they waved off their loved ones, many of them never to return.

The Victory Parade in 1945. When Oldham first acquired its police force in the 1850s it had one superintendent, one sergeant and ten constables. Qualifications for the job were a minimum standing height of 5 feet 8 inches without shoes, plus the ability to read and write. The force kept law and order only in the daytime and during the night this duty was taken over by the night watchman.

Uniformed organisations file past the mayor and officials outside the Town Hall for the Victory Parade of 1945.

Sailors salute and celebrate the end of the Second World War in the Victory Parade.

Nurses parade in the same 1945 procession on their way to a thanksgiving service.

George Street Independent Methodist Boys Brigade 19th Oldham. Third from right in the front row is Jimmy Mottley, who was both leader and mentor to the boys for many years. He was also a knocker-up from 1923 until 1961 when he gave up, feeling that he had been defeated by modern alarm clocks. He worked from 4.30 a.m. until 7.00 a.m. to knock up his 400 customers. When the war came he simply donned a tin helmet. He charged one penny a visit and the cost never altered in thirty-eight years.

Whit Walks in 1900.

George Street on Whit Friday 1913.

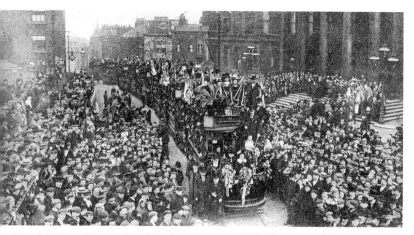

The celebration of the opening of the electric tramways, 1900. The service of through trams from Manchester to Oldham was delayed while the Manchester cars were fitted with brakes which were suitable for the hill climb. The first tram from Manchester was driven into Oldham by the Lord Mayor of Manchester.

The visit of King George V and Queen Mary in 1913. Schoolchildren were taken to Werneth Park in special trams. 'At long last the royal car appeared and we had to wave our flags and everyone was getting poked in the eye and that and we'd waited for ages and it was over in a minute. We would have liked to be let loose in the park a bit after that – but we had to go. Looking back, it was a bit of a let-down. I didn't think she looked like a Queen a bit – just a posh lady really.'

Members of Oldham Parish Church walk through the town centre on a wet Whit Friday in the 1950s.

The Mayoral procession in 1974. Councillor Ellen Brierley JP was the first Mayor when Oldham became a Metropolitan Borough Council. On her left is her sister Hilda who was the Mayoress.

Three

Happenings

Civil Defence operations always drew the crowds. Here in 1947 the CD practice rescuing someone from the top of the Palladium Cinema, which stood next to the library. Was the title of the film showing at the time just a mere coincidence?

King George V and Queen Mary's visit to Oldham in 1913. The royal procession is seen here on Yorkshire Street.

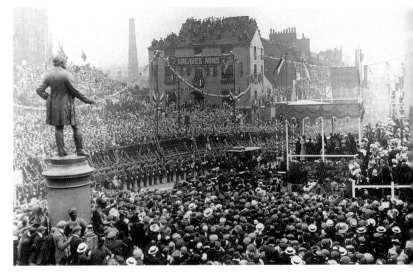

The same visit of King George V and Queen Mary in 1913. Thousands of Oldham people gathered in the centre of the town to catch a glimpse. John Platt, on his pedestal near the Town Hall, got the best view of all.

The Duke of Gloucester visits Oldham in the 1930s.

Rain greeted the Queen when she came to Oldham in 1954. This photograph shows her arrival at the Town Hall with the Duke of Edinburgh.

Children at Clarksfield School tending their garden, *c.* 1911.

The Beautiful Oldham Society was created by a small band of idealists headed by Mary Higgs. They were inspired by a book entitled Garden Cities of Tomorrow published in 1902 which advocated the building of houses which could be purchased at a reasonable cost and would give local people a better standard of living. The scheme received help from Mrs Charles Lees of Werneth Park, who owned the land. On an area of fifty acres it was planned to build 700 houses at an average cost of £230 each. The area became known as the Garden Suburbs and this photograph shows a tree-planting ceremony to commemorate the occasion. Margery Lees inherited Werneth Park from her parents. A Suffragette, she never married, and on her death bequeathed Werneth Park to the people of Oldham.

Clarksfield School, *c.* 1911. The little girl with two ringlets on the front row at the left, is Annie Holden.

The St Domingo Street school was attached to the Wesleyan church and opened its doors to children of the churchgoers. It was schools such as this one which produced exquisite samplers, started when the child began school and taken home when completed. In the beginning the teachers had little or no education themselves and no equipment; it is to their credit that they produced some wonderful scholars.

Every drama brings the crowds. In this one, of 22 April 1907, a train has left the sidings line alongside the Werneth Incline which had a gradient of 1 in 27. A crane is attempting to lift the wagon and the engine lies in the roadway. The view looks towards Cowhill.

Hathershaw Mill fire on 15 February 1907. This fire burned for days and the damage was estimated at £60,000. Iris Mill was built on the same site later the same year.

A closer view of the railway smash at Cowhill, Oldham on 22 April 1907.

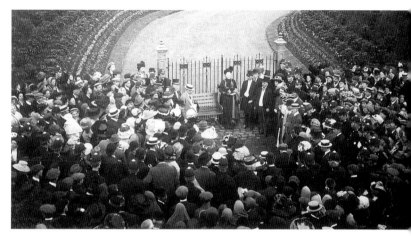

The opening of Copsterhill Park in June 1911 by Mrs Lees who was, at that time, the Mayor of Oldham. The area covers over sixteen acres with bowling greens, tennis courts, a playground and playing field.

The opening of the Palace Theatre in 1908. Mary Marron is the little girl on the left who assisted her father, the man raising his hat on the right, by turning over the numbers after each act. When the Palace was built, Oldham had for the first time a luxurious music hall, with a wonderful balcony decorated in red and gold. In the corridor leading down to the stalls was an enormous painting of Vesta Tilley, a well known artiste of her day, who later became Lady De-Frece. Eventually the people who had loved the Palace were left only with their memories of the thrills and laughter, the mingled smells of oranges from the gallery and cigars from the stalls, the memory of the ending of the overture, the dimming of the lights and the swish of the splendid crimson and gold curtain – it closed in 1935 and the Odeon cinema was built in its place. The Odeon too has now gone, and the site stands empty.

Oldham Microscopical Society, *c.* 1920s; pond dipping.

After the storm at the Orme Mill, Waterhead, in July 1927. Flooding resulted in the foundation brickwork giving way to a depth of eighteen feet. The force of water was so powerful that it washed away the bridge near the Orme, bursting the tunnel and causing the culvert which passed under the mill to collapse.

The end of a livelihood: Victoria Market in ruins after the fire of October 1974.

The annual baby show, Werneth Park, 1914. Every year baby shows were held at the park and areas would be represented by the babies that came from them. This is a group from Grosvenor Street. Sadly, some of these children would undoubtedly lose their fathers in the war which was to come.

A day out for Robinson's grocers of the Market Hall and their colleagues. It was the Tradesman's Holiday. Tuesday was half-day closing for shopkeepers except for once a year when they had a full day. The engineering trade had Mechanics' Yearly Day which was on a Saturday, once a year.

Another photograph of the opening of the Garden Suburbs in August 1909 illustrating that, however important the occasion, wherever the water, there the boys will be.

Brownie Revels in Alexandra Park, c. 1946.

A captive audience during a Home Guard exercise in 1942.

Oldham Civil Defence team in 1956. This photograph shows the Emergency Feeding Team with their improvised boiling plate and double-dustbin oven cooker which they built during the CD competition semi-finals.

The opening of the first prefabricated house built by Oldham Council in September 1946. The house was in Tweed Road, Primrose Bank and the first tenants were Mr and Mrs Charles Sullivan and their daughter Margaret. The keys were presented to them by the Mayor, Alderman Stirling Marron, who performed the opening ceremony. Mr Sullivan had served in the Navy during the Second World War and, like many young ex-servicemen who married during the war or just after peace was declared, had no home in which to rear a young family. As the weeks went by, more and more of these temporary houses were provided by Oldham Council and a steady housing programme began to take place.

The tramway service in Oldham came to an end on 3 August 1946. Oldhamers lined the streets for their farewell tribute and children placed pennies on the tramlines to keep for souvenirs. The Mayor, Alderman Stirling Marron, drove the last tram through the town.

The 'Topping Out' ceremony of the Civic Centre took place on 18 June 1976. The mayor at the time was Councillor Christopher McCall. 'Topping Out' signifies that the building has reached its highest point and the tradition goes back beyond mediaeval times. The actual ceremony differs throughout the world, and, although the motive varies, it has survived for many hundreds of years and is usually a gesture of goodwill between client and builder.

Four

The Changing Face of Oldham

The Market Place in about 1948 showing the construction of the new roundabout system. The imposing building at the top of West Street is the Prince William of Gloucester Hotel, commonly known as the Top Drum. On the opposite corner is the Crown Hotel on Cheapside which was back-to-back with the Crown and Anchor on Henshaw Street. Because they were adjacent and to avoid confusion, people would say 'I'll meet you at the C and A', which was a curious thing as when the two pubs were demolished, C&A outfitters was built in their place. It would be nearly thirty years later that the Civic Centre appeared on the skyline.

During the period 1934-5, Oldham Council exercised a huge clearance campaign. This and the following photograph show the Mount Pleasant area, outside toilets, poor sanitation but a wealth of community spirit which disappeared with the new high-rise buildings.

'Morning chat' – today it would be 'morning coffee'.

Market Hotel on Curzon Street in about 1912. The men are Oldham Brewery draymen, who have just completed a delivery. Fred Barratt sat on the centre barrel and Peter Beaumont with the horse. The Halifax Building Society is now on this site.

Mumps in the 1920s. The Salisbury Hotel is on the left, just before Mumps Bridge.

In 1975 Central Baths on Union Street were the oldest baths still in use in Britain, having been opened in 1854. The 'duck-pond' as it was affectionately called, was the learners' pool and this photograph shows some children having their last splash before the building closed down. Facilities at the building had become out-dated, pools were the wrong size for competitions and the private baths were not in demand any more. 'We used to go to the private baths on our way home from work on Fridays because we had no bathroom then. Sometimes you had to wait your turn, it was so busy. It was 4d with a piece of soap (carbolic), and a towel like cardboard – six inches of water that was tepid and yet nobody grumbled'.

The High Street around 1910 before road widening made the demolition of the George Hotel necessary. The George was replaced by Wild's jewellers. Later, in the same place, have been Weaver to Wearer, the 50/- tailors, John Colliers and, today, the Bradford and Bingley Building Society. Below is a rough sketch, which is not drawn to scale, but shows the changes which took place.

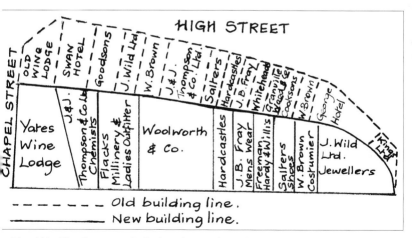

HIGH STREET

CHAPEL STREET

Old building line.

New building line.

The old building line was set back, the widest part being thirty feet, narrowing to eighteen feet. All the work was undertaken by local firms. The broken line shows the positions of the old shops and the solid line, the edges of the new ones. Work began in 1912 but had to be postponed due to the outbreak of war in 1914. Because of this delay, rebuilding was still going on in the 1920s.

The idea of the Mechanics Institute was first fostered at a meeting in April 1865 at St John's School, Werneth. Oldham's industrial magnates were behind the idea. The Institute was opened in Manchester Street in 1867 by Mr Gladstone and cost £1,500. It became an educational centre for apprentices, especially from Platt Brothers, who attended a few hours each day.

People stop and stare as the car cheekily competes with the tram in the Market Place in about 1920.

Rhodes Bank, *c.* 1910. On the left can be seen the YMCA which is next door to, and over the top of Arthur Goss, gentlemen's outfitters. The building on the corner is the General Clothing Club office, now the *Oldham Chronicle* building.

The Albion Hotel, Nos 1–3 High Street, situated at the corner of the High Street and Curzon Street. When a syndicate of local businessmen and innkeepers was formed to discuss purchasing Oldham Brewery in 1873 they met in this building and drew up details of an offer and a limited company. Oldham Brewery bought the hotel in 1897 and rebuilt it in 1937. During the Second World War it became very popular for entertainment. It was sold to developers in 1972 for conversion into retail shops.

A Whit Sunday in the 1920s and a group of people assemble to sing at the Market Place. The Sunday school banner leans against the wall.

The top of George Street in the 1920s, once a busy shopping street but now demolished. The People's Cash Chemists building has had a varied life; it was once Weston's Ladies Wear and Phil Cohen's, the tailors.

Ford Bakery, Hathershaw Lane, c. 1935. Hilda Stapleton remembers 'I used to pass this building every morning on the way to school with my sister. Mr Keegan, the manager, would be stood at the gate. "Good morning twins", he would say. "Good morning, Sir," we replied. We weren't twins but we were always dressed the same. I started work here in 1930 when I was fourteen. All the malt loaves were wrapped by hand; in fact most of the cake was just like home-made. I worked from 7.00 a.m.–7.00 p.m.' Ford's was eventually bought by a Stockport company but in the late thirties was closed completely. Park Cake Bakery purchased the building early in 1940 before they started business on the Honeywell Mill site.

Right: The Empire Theatre on Waterloo Street was opened in June 1897. The land was about thirty feet below street level and the entrance had a flight of stone steps to the auditorium. It was the only theatre built in Oldham which had exits on four sides and, more important still, it was lit throughout by electricity. The Empire had an illustrious career before the sad march of time took its toll. Music-hall, pantomimes, concerts, plays and variety-shows all appeared there and it was the building which showed the first silent film in Oldham in 1911 and, proudly, the first 'talkie' in 1929. After a long spell as a cinema, the theatre went 'live' again at the beginning of the Second World War and people queued in the blackout to see their favourite performers. By 1955 it was once again a cinema, except for the occasional special performance featuring a well-known star. The Empire finally closed in 1969 and the site now stands empty.

Huddersfield Road at the turn of the century showing Leathley's Decorators at Nos 2 and 4.

Yorkshire Street decked out for the Coronation celebrations in 1937.

The Fish Market, Albion Street in 1931. It was demolished in 1938 and a modern fish shop with adjoining properties replaced it.

The High Street in the early 1950s. The Co-operative café is above their shop, next to Boots the chemists. Ellwood's fabric shop can be seen on the left next to the Yorkshire Penny Bank.

The Mumps area in 1961, just before the hammer fell. Andymans Stores advertises the new Formica.

Looking down on the old Town Hall from the Oldham Parish Church tower in 1900, before the cenotaph was built.

The corner of Hartley Street and Pembroke Street around 1900. The man in the background is carrying two stone bottles which would contain herb beer or sarsaparilla, renewable once a week for a few pence when the cart came round. In winter these would often be used as hot water bottles.

'Just off to Sunday School' in Brompton Street in 1910. 'Our Joe didn't want to be on the photo, so he stood in the road. We took Emily's sister with us everywhere and when we were playing out we often sat her on the window-bottom to watch us. I suppose it's a miracle that she never fell off!'

Above: Excavation for the St Peter's precinct which was never popular and was christened 'Windy City' by local people. The area in the photograph once held St Peter's church, the Technical School, offices and a number of houses which faced St Peter Street.

Left: The corner of George Street, looking into St Peter Street. St Peter's church can be seen behind the lamp. Yates's Wine Lodge is visible in the distance on the left.

Manchester Street in the 1920s.

The shopping area and subway in Market Place in the late 1970s.

The Salvation Army Citadel was opened in 1886 by General William Booth, founder of the Salvation Army. It accommodated 2,000 people and was often full! Sadly, it was disposed of in 1968 due to the need of drastic structural repairs. At one time it was said to have the best brass band in the North-West.

A bird's eye view of the extent of the market stalls, c. 1960. The area to the right of the centre is now the Sports Centre, while the roof top of the old Victoria Market is visible near the top of the photograph on the left.

The cotton famine of the 1860s created chronic unemployment in Oldham as well as in other cotton towns. By 1863 a committee had been formed and, with the help of a government loan and the purchase of land at Swine Clough, the creation of a park was planned. One condition laid down by the Revd John Cocker of Crompton, from whom the land was purchased, was that the unemployed cotton operatives were to be used as a labour force. Alexandra Park was opened on 28 August 1865 by the mayor at that time who was Josiah Radcliffe; the park was named to commemorate the recent marriage of the Prince of Wales to Princess Alexandra of Denmark.

The refreshment room in Alexandra Park was built in 1865, just in time for the park's official opening ceremony. The aim was to have a continental style café on the ground floor and a museum on the upper floor. The latter was never achieved but the café continued to be a popular meeting place on Sunday afternoons for the young people of Oldham until it fell into disrepair and was demolished in 1955.

Delivering a last prayer before demolition. The magnificent St Peter's church stands forlorn. The first St Peter's church was built in 1768. It was pulled down in 1899 because it wasn't big enough to take the congregation and the Parish church was always full. Wild, Collins and Wild were the architects appointed to design the new St Peter's, which was consecrated in 1901. The church was demolished in 1967 to make way for the new St Peter's precinct. The remains of the people in the graveyard were removed to Greenacres cemetery.

A procession to celebrate the Jubilee of Incorporation in 1899. So many people took part that it is remarkable there were any spectators. Oldham had achieved many goals since the town was granted its Charter in 1849. Among these wonderful things were an art gallery, free libraries, a technical school, swimming baths, a gasworks, hospitals, a grammar school and fire stations. Oldham people had every reason to be proud.

Every occasion was once celebrated with a large bonfire on Oldham Edge. This one was in the early summer of 1913 to celebrate the visit of King George V, Queen Mary and Prince Albert, who became King George VI.

Union Street Methodist chapel was built in 1875 and became Oldham's premier Methodist church. It was built for 900 people. The early Methodists in Oldham, at the beginning of the nineteenth century, met in a doctor's house in Cannon Street, from which they were asked to leave because their singing was too noisy. When the chapel was demolished, the front arches were used as an entrance to the new offices built in its place.

York Castle, *c. 1970* before demolition. Joseph Ball, who built York Castle in 1883, was a steeplejack who started his own business when he was married at only sixteen years of age. At eight years old he began his first dangerous job as a climber of chimneys. In his time he controlled one of the most important specialist businesses in the United Kingdom and was responsible for the correcting and repair of many of Oldham's mill chimneys. He planned to open a theatre at York Castle but the council refused to pass the plans. Instead, he took over the Gaiety Theatre in Union Street, which later became the Victory Cinema. In the 1960s a film crew came to Oldham to make a film of Joe's life. It is reputed that he made a fortune. .

Opposite above: Oldham Central Library, Union Street, *c.* 1900. Before open access, the reader had to request the book of his choice; browsing was not allowed. Sometimes it was possible to point to the one requested. Instructions were fastened to panels along with large notices saying, 'Quiet Please!'

Opposite below: Oldham Art Gallery around 1900. In the background can be seen the popular and dramatic painting of the *Death of Cleopatra* by the Hon. John Collier before it was damaged. The painting was thought to have been slashed by a militant suffragette. It was kept in storage for many years until the late 1980s when it was restored to its former grandeur by painting conservators

Looking towards the Star Inn in the 1950s. On the right is the Duke of Edinburgh public house, with the Electraceum cinema in the middle of the row with Clegg's opticians. The Antelope Inn is on the left, at the top of Park Street; also in view is the King Street Independent Methodist tower.

Werneth Fire Station decorated for the Coronation of King George VI in 1937. The building stood at the corner of Manchester Street and Frederick Street; beyond this junction Manchester Street became Manchester Road. The fire station was built in 1897 and demolished in March 1989.

Opposite above: During the popularity of the bicycle in the early years of the twentieth century, Ralph Eglin snr. had a cycle shop on Yorkshire Street. Many people were talking about the various models of cars slowly appearing on the market and Ralph became interested in going into the motor-car business. Along with six friends, who included two rope manufacturers, two people in the cotton trade, a butcher and a confectioner, he formed the Oldham Motor Company in 1907. The building in this photograph was the first that they acquired and was rented. It stood at the corner of Manchester Road and Oxford Street, opposite Werneth Fire Station.

Opposite below: By 1911 the directors of the Oldham Motor Company had agreed to take a plot of land in Manchester Street and five shops and a garage were established. That same year it was decided that the company would take on the Ford agency. Just before this building was demolished for road widening, they moved to the opposite side of the road on the site of the Werneth Mill, which they already owned.

The Oldham Motor Co. Ltd., Werneth

Motor Engineers and Repairers.

SOLE AGENTS

DAIMLER,
SUNBEAM,
FIAT,
TALBOT,
FORD,
AUSTIN,
B.S.A.,
BRITAIN,

CARS.

AGENTS for ..

MICHELIN,
DUNLOP,
GOODRICH,
PALMER,
SKEW,

TYRES.

OPEN AND CLOSED CARS FOR HIRE.

We Overhaul, Repair, Paint, and Re-Upholster any make of Car.

TELEGRAMS: "Motors, Oldham."   TELEPHONE: 1301; Taxi Stand, 1384.

Manchester Street in 1967. The fire station can be seen on the left and Werneth Mill adjoining is partly razed. The building of the new flats has begun and the extent of the Oldham Motor Company, proudly displaying the Ford emblem, is evident.

The Oldham Infirmary foundation stone was laid in April 1870 but the hospital was not completed until over two years later; the official opening took place in September 1872. Florence Nightingale, who was prevented from accepting her invitation due to illness, sent a letter of apology. It became the Royal Infirmary by the gracious permission of King George V on 20 March 1911. After it was demolished, the Sixth Form College was built in its place.

Oldham from Waterhead in the 1920s. Taken at the end of August when the mills were closed for Oldham Wakes, the sky is clear of smoke from the chimneys. The area at the front of the photograph is now built upon.

Five

Work and Play

Dinner time at Platt Brothers, Featherstall Road, in the 1930s. The people of Oldham could set their clocks by Platts' whistle. Before the advent of canteens most people went home for dinner. Platts were famous throughout the world for their manufacture of textile machines. The company gave employment to a force of workmen that was probably the largest compared to any other local firm. In fact, Platts gained many prestigious awards from all over the world. John Platt became the sole owner of Platts after the death of his brother, James, in a shooting accident on the moors in 1857 and also by his marriage to the daughter of Elijah Hibbert, who was his father's partner.

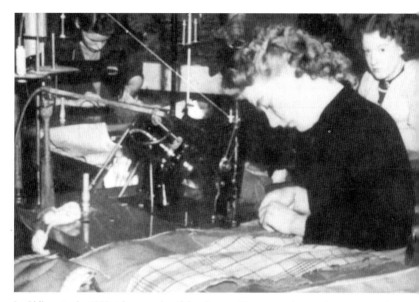

In Oldham in the 1950s jobs were plentiful and every effort was made to entice young people into a variety of industries. These two advertisements were featured in an Oldham youth magazine. This one was for Weatherlux (Manchester) Ltd, rainwear manufacturers.

Oldham advertisement in the 1950s for Medlock Manufacturing Company Ltd.

Hugh Gaitskell visiting Oldham during a fact-finding tour of Lancashire in September 1958. Here he talks to some girls in a local cotton mill at lunch time.

Mill Canteen in the 1950s.

Because of labour shortages due to the conscription of postmen during the First World War, it was decided to employ women. This happy breed are photographed on Greaves Street in March 1914 outside the General Post Office, which is now the Local Studies Library and Oldham Museum.

The sorting department of the General Post Office on Union Street in the 1930s.

Above: 'Picking the winners'. A lunch time break behind the scenes of the General Post Office at the corner of Union Street and Greaves Street, also in the 1930s.

Right: 'After a hard day's work! The last batch of mail gone and must get organised for the next shift – just have forty winks first!'

Star Iron Works, Greenacres Road, c. 1909, owned by William Toole. Tooles was a family concern which manufactured iron fireplaces, wringing machines and grids for street drainage. The grids carried the name of Toole, and across the bottom Greenacres. In 1891 the firm described themselves as 'Iron Fence and Palisading Makers'! William Toole lived locally at No.175 Greenacres Road, which was usual during that time.

Laying the tram lines looking towards Mumps Bridge in 1901. The new tram-shed, later to become the bus garage, is under construction on the left.

Oldham built its first wash-house in 1915 at Robin Hill. Cedar Street, where this photograph was taken, was built in 1925 and the third one was built at Hollinwood in 1932. They were not just somewhere to do the washing; they were places where the community was kept alive.

The construction of the boating lake in Alexandra Park in 1903 cost the enormous sum of £14,000, but at the time it became one of the main attractions. This photograph shows the building of a new landing stage in the 1930s.

The building of John Hall's Foundry in about 1910. George Holdsworth is on the scaffolding with a bucket.

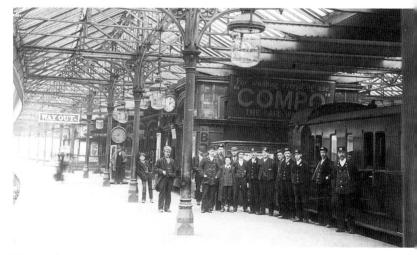

Mumps railway station around 1900. 'The station clock had to be always right. I didn't have a watch so I had nothing to check it with and it was my job. I had to stand on ladders and Mr Walsh would look at his Albert, which he always wore'.

'I always wanted to go upstairs on the tram and if I was with my Dad, he let me. It was wonderful to look down on the horses and carts and everything. Sometimes, if a bike-rider wasn't careful, he would slide into the tram lines and it was difficult to get out – it nearly always ended up with him having to get off his bike and pulling it free!'

Shafts of sunlight shine on the work force at the Star Iron Works. The building on Greenacres Road still stands and although the frontage in white brick proudly displays the words 'Wm. Toole, Star Iron Works', it is now owned by B. & H. Machine Tools Ltd, trading under the name of B. & H. Gears.

An East Lancashire & Oldham Carrying Company steam wagon around 1905.

Mr Lambert delivering milk for the Co-op ('3½d per quart and full dividend') in a photograph taken outside Alexandra Park gates. The boy's name was Ellis and the horse was called *Dancer*.

The Lancashire Cotton Corporation tested for all the forty eight mills in its group, many of which were in Oldham. The Central Testing and Quality Control Department was located at Thornycroft until 1969 when it moved to the Heron Mill.

The Lancashire Cotton Corporation had taken over Thornycroft, a robust but refined building on the Coppice, in 1960. Before this it was a private school run by two sisters – the Misses Mellodew – who had decided to retire and buy a smaller house. The above room was once a classroom and in the 1960s housed the loom, pictured here, which was used for looking at the condition of yarn tested. Thornycroft now belongs to Hulme Grammar School.

Another view of tram-line laying. This time the lines go towards Union Street and Yorkshire Street. The Oldham Hotel can be seen on the right.

Covering the cobbles on Rochdale Road in 1949. This lorry is loading tarmac onto a laying machine. It took quite a few years to cover the cobbles and tram lines to make it easier for buses to travel.

Celebrating the beginning of Prudential Assurance in Oldham. As spectators gather on Union Street, the first arch can just be seen on the right and the boarding above the platform of VIPs has the name W. Jones, Oldham's first mayor in 1849, together with that of J. Brierley, mayor in 1899. This gives us some idea of the date of the photograph, although the completed Prudential building didn't open until 1901. Priory Mill is on the left. The mill did not cease production until 1920 when, with alterations, it was converted into offices and became known as the Priory Buildings.

Wellington Street School, *c.* 1910. Children line up to file into school. The building, which was at the top of Wellington Street and Park Road, was built in 1878. Its life as a school lasted until 1930. It was badly ventilated, the rooms were very small with high ceilings and no width. After it closed as a school it was used by the Women's Institute and at the outbreak of the Second World War in 1939, it fulfilled a dual role when the British Restaurant was opened on the ground floor. In 1946 it once again reverted back to a school – this time the School of Commerce with evening classes offering all academic subjects. It closed, 'in the name of progress', in July 1966.

Clarksfield School in 1908. Physical training, as it was called, is taking place in the hall. PT lessons were never combined with the girls who then, as an alternative, did sewing.

The Bluecoat School opened in 1834 and was then a boys-only school, many of them boarders. Most of the pupils were either orphans or children of the widowed, often rescued from poverty and squalor and the stigma that accompanied them. Although lacking in the support of a loving family, the boys were clothed and fed and received regular medical examinations. Their education was of the very best and their schooling took them to their fourteenth birthday. Every boy was found a job that suited his aptitude and many gained excellent professional qualifications. Unfortunately, the founder, Mr Thomas Henshaw, did not even live to see the foundation stone laid in 1829. He was found drowned in 1810 in a reservoir near the hat manufacturers business that he had worked to establish. In July 1952, the school was no longer residential and was converted into a secondary modern school. In July 1966 the new extensions were opened by Sir Frank Lord and by September of the same year, along with many other schools in Oldham, the Bluecoat became a comprehensive school.

Oldham YMCA Rugby Football Club in 1910.

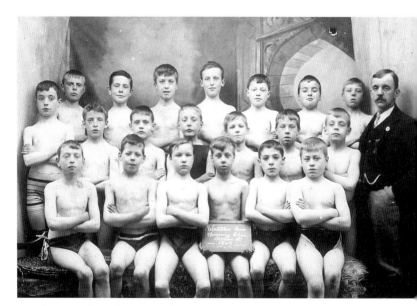

Waterloo Council School swimming class in 1907.

A keep fit class in 1948 at the YMCA which was at Rhodes Bank. The association catered for many activities and competitions, including table-tennis and chess, for both sexes.

The Oldham Citizens Club fancy dress party, Christmas Eve, 1947.

Oldham Ladies Swimming Club, c. 1912 at Waterhead Baths. Second from the left on the back row is May Whitehead and on the extreme right, at the back, is Mary Critchley. On the extreme left in the middle row is Mrs Brierley, whose husband had the photographer's business on Union Street.

The paddling pool in Werneth Park, 24 August 1959. The park was presented to the town by Marjory Lees and was formally opened by the Mayor, Alderman J.R. Bainbridge on 30 May 1936. Many local societies who were active in arts and crafts were eager to use the conservatory and music room. During the Second World War the huge lawn was ploughed and vegetables were grown for food production.

Oldham Motor Cycling Club, c. 1911, outside Alexandra Park gates. The baby in the centre is Bessie, a member of the Sinkinson family who lived at Abbeyhills House and owned the King Street Mill, which burned down in 1908. The Grand Theatre was built in its place and it subsequently became the Gaumont Cinema.

Alexandra Park on a Sunday afternoon in the 1920s. 'All the conservatories would be open and they were full of exotic blooms and the smell was wonderful but it was so hot and we weren't allowed to take our jackets off – it was Sunday you see'.

'We used to set off right after breakfast with sandwiches. It was always busier after three o'clock on Sundays when the Sunday schools finished. Then it got really packed. With the uncertain weather we get, it couldn't possibly survive but there has never been anything like Grotton Lido before or since.'

Skating on Alexandra Park lake, c. 1900. This was always a precarious pastime, some people here look more confident than others!

Excelsior Cycling Club in 1914, outside the Up Steps Hotel, High Street. The members called themselves the Monks of St Bernard.

Alexandra Park lake in 1979. The launch is advertising the Oldham Summer Show which was held once a year in the park, with side-shows, displays and many other activities.

The Girls Friendly Society on holiday in the 1950s. Their headquarters were at St Thomas's church, Werneth.

The Palladium Cinema, Union Street, featuring *Gone with the Wind* in June 1943. Although cinema going was always popular during that time, the film, which lasted for three hours and forty minutes, drew audiences never before recorded.

Strawberry Gardens, Glodwick, *c.* 1890. At this time the gardens were owned by John and James Cheetham who lived there with their families. The Cheethams were florists and nurserymen who used their talents to build up a lucrative business. The gardens had conservatories, a gymnasium, tea rooms and many flowers and plants. On Sunday afternoons it was popular with families who could take a picnic and spend the whole day there. The free admission and surrounding fields both added to the attraction. In the thirties the number of visitors fell and the tea rooms stood abandoned, belonging to another age, until 1960. Attractive modern housing is now built on the area.

Alexandra Park Lake, *c.* 1905, with the magnificent Park Road cotton warehouses on the horizon. Although derelict, the building still proudly stands, a reminder of an industrious town.

Six

Putting it to Bed

On the first day of the electricity cuts on Friday 11 February 1972, the *Oldham Evening Chronicle* was finished, ready for despatch.

The British Empire Exhibition at Wembley in 1924.

Oldham once relied on Manchester for its local news. The *Manchester Guardian* had an Oldham reporter, the historian Edwin Butterworth. He had some very forthright opinions and knew exactly what the Oldham people wanted to read about. Nevertheless, when the *Chronicle* was created in 1854, the year that the Crimean war began, it was greeted with immense warmth by the local population. It started life at No. 22 Yorkshire Street, which then became a printers and stationers. The building is now occupied by a building society.

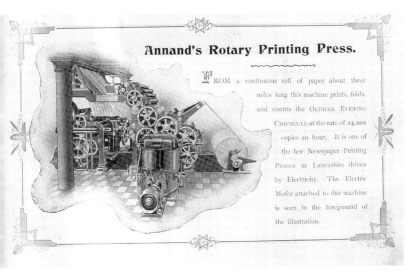

Annand's Rotary Printing Press.

FROM a continuous roll of paper about three miles long this machine prints, folds, and counts the OLDHAM EVENING CHRONICLE at the rate of 24,000 copies an hour. It is one of the few Newspaper Printing Presses in Lancashire driven by Electricity. The Electric Motor attached to this machine is seen in the foreground of the illustration.

In the early 1900s, from a continuous roll of paper around three miles in length, this machine could print, fold and count the newspaper at a rate of 24,000 copies an hour.

In 1920, as the company expanded and successfully grew, it was decided that a move to larger premises would be an advantage. It was then that Hirst and Rennie were joined by Mr Clarence Kidd who was the head of a firm of printers, Samuel Fish Ltd, on Ascroft Street. He became a joint managing-director and was still with the *Chronicle* in this magnificent building, No.172 Union Street, when it celebrated its centenary in 1954. The BU on the cars represented the Oldham registration numbers – no parking tickets!

Opposite above: This building was next to the Palace Theatre, at the corner of Bridge Street and was occupied by the *Chronicle* from 1889 to 1923. It was here that they celebrated the Coronation of King Edward VII on 9 August 1902. It was sold to Times Printers in 1923 and is now Kwikprint stationers.

Opposite below: This was the rotary printing press used by the *Chronicle* in about 1923. Compared with today's huge colour printing-press which fills three floors of the press hall in Union Street, it is a minnow.

Stories and advertisements were set in lines of type by compositors seated at Linotype machines. These typesetting machines were the new technology of their day in the 1890s. They replaced men who set each letter by hand. Using the Linotype machine, whole lines of type could be set in lead and then made up into pages. This picture, taken in the early 1920s, shows the *Chronicle*'s row of Linotype machines and, on the left, the pneumatic-tube system used for sending messages and copy around the building.

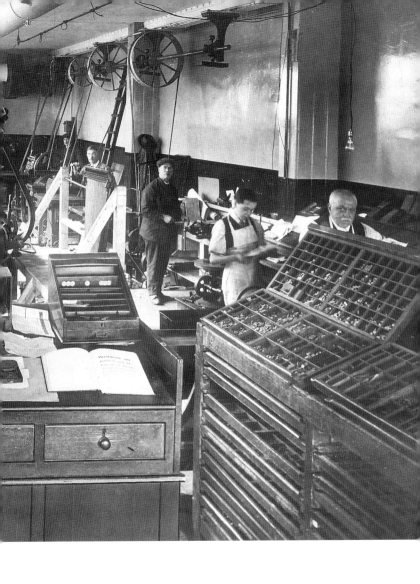

In the 1920s national news was received by telegram from news agencies such as the Press Association and Reuters. These were received and printed on tape at high speed. The messages were then stuck up on to sheets; further messages could be sent back by using a morse key. What was amazing was that people who used the machines could actually read the news as it was coming through.

The *Oldham Evening Chronicle* has always organised trips which have become more ambitious as time has gone by. This is April 1922 – The Green Final outing to London from the Featherstall and Junction pubs. They went there and back in this bone-shaker.

The Green Final Amateur Bowling Championship, Alexandra Park, 1929.

The *Chronicle*'s offices at No.172 Union Street were not specifically built for the company, though they were extensively refurbished. Earlier pictures show a clothing club and insurance company occupying the building. In the 1920s the *Chronicle* even had a commissionaire to greet customers.

No such thing as open-plan offices in 1923! This photograph of the editorial department was taken just after the *Chronicle* moved to its present home in Union Street. Standing at the desk framed by the doorway is the editor of the time, William S. Stewart, the newspaper's longest serving editor. He was in charge from 1917 until 1946 and, in fact, worked for the company for fifty-two years, having started as a printer's devil.

All set for delivery to newsagents throughout Oldham.

This is the news room in 1953. The woman is Hilda Williams, who wrote the women's page. Jimmy Bennett, chief sub-editor, is on the right. It was his job to decide what stories would be used. He was also the editor of *Lancashire Miscellany*, a collection of dialect poetry.

Reporters writing stories in 1953.

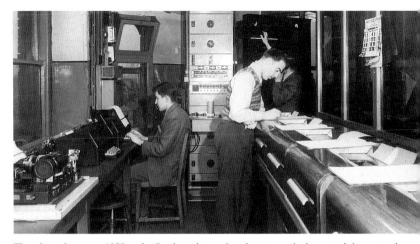

The telegraph room – 1950s style. On the right are the teleprinters which received the national news from the Press Association. On the left is the machine to return messages.

Coming home from the Centenary trip to Symonds Yat, 9 May 1954.

Setting display advertising. A border surrounded each advert, made up of separate elements of type, then string was tied very tightly round everything and the whole display lifted up with baited breath. It was rather like lifting a jigsaw puzzle and was quite a feat because, if it collapsed, it had to be started all over again.

Directors on the *Chronicle*'s Centenary trip in May 1954. Included in the photograph are Henry Hirst, Clarence Kidd, Tommy Lloyd and John Hirst.

Left: The *Chronicle* acquires a clock which soon became a landmark.

Below: Kenneth Hirst, editor of the *Oldham Evening Chronicle* from 1959–1982, skating on the roof of the YMCA in January 1954. He was a wonderful, talented man who would have a go at many things and succeeded at most of them.

Opposite: Papers coming off the Hoe and Crabtree press which was used from 1947–1991.

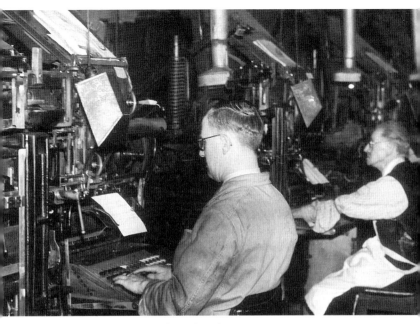

Close-up of Linotype operators who also work in the news room.

Opposite above: During the newspaper strike in June 1959. This was a national protest, not a local one. Harry Hirst remembers, 'John [Hirst] ran the rotary press on his own during the strike and cast the plates as well. It was an amazing task. Nobody else in the office could have done it. He really understood those machines. If it hadn't been for that, there would have been no newspaper at all – we had nothing but admiration for him.'

Opposite below: Again, during the 1959 strike, the directors and apprentices at work on the production of the *Oldham Evening Chronicle*. Kenneth Hirst and Tommy Lloyd are working on the stone where the pages were made up.

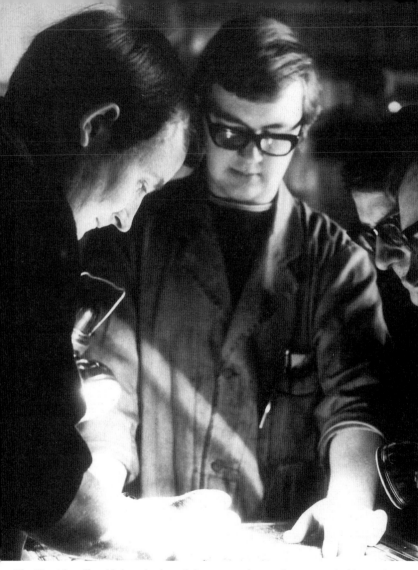

The *Chronicle* staff could always be depended upon to make sure the town received its evening paper. This photograph shows work going on during one of the power cuts in 1970. After this, it was decided that the firm should buy its own generator. Included in the photograph are Keith Wolfenden, Derek Sarsfield, Gordon Maxwell and Barry Hughes.

Demolishing the Roscoe Mill chimney in 1972. The building is now used by Hirst, Kidd & Rennie for commercial printing.

Demolition of the old building in the 1970s was carried out in two stages. This photograph shows the first destruction in June 1970.

Above: By 23 November 1971, progress with the new structure can be seen, with part of the old building still in use but earmarked for demolition.

Right: The *Oldham Evening Chronicle*'s new building in 1974. Though the Rhodes Bank and Mumps area is quite different from when the *Chronicle* first moved here, this is still Oldham's centre of local and national news.

Looking down on an Oldham once familiar to many of us. The view is from Oldham parish church, with the old Radclyffe Arms pub centre right and a ghostly sighting of the Bluecoat School at the top left. While the rows and rows of back-to-back terraced houses nudge each other, we are reminded of how many lives must have intertwined in those days.

Acknowledgements

I wish to thank the following people
who have contributed to the compilation of this book
in a variety of ways and especially
for the loan of precious family photographs:

Keith Adams,
Pat Bottomley for selflessly giving her time to type the captions, Margaret Eastham,
The Eglins of Oldham Motor Company, Peter Fox,
Harry Hirst, Philip Hirst of the *Oldham Chronicle* for interest and involvement,
Oldham Local Studies Library for the loan of photographs from their collection,
Joyce Pearson, Vivien Pellowe, Hilda Stapleton, Geoff Woodhead,
and all the people who have, and still are,
adding to the illustrious photographic archive of Oldham.

I acknowledge copyright of the extract (page 19)
reproduced from the 1973 edition of the *Goad Plan*
under licence from Charles Goad Ltd, Hatfield, Herts,
which immediately reminds us of our changing town.